P9-BYA-193

DOVER·THRIFT·EDITIONS

World War One British Poets

BROOKE, OWEN, SASSOON, ROSENBERG AND OTHERS

EDITED BY

CANDACE WARD

DOVER PUBLICATIONS, INC.
Mineola, New York

DOVER THRIFT EDITIONS

GENERAL EDITOR: STANLEY APPELBAUM
EDITOR OF THIS VOLUME: CANDACE WARD

Bibliographical Note

World War One British Poets: Brooke, Owen, Sassoon, Rosenberg and Others is a new anthology, first published by Dover Publications, Inc., in 1997.

Library of Congress Cataloging-in-Publication Data

World War One British poets : Brooke, Owen, Sassoon, Rosenberg, and others / edited by Candace Ward.
    p.   cm. — (Dover thrift editions)
  ISBN 0-486-29568-0 (pbk.)
  1. English poetry — 20th century. 2. World War, 1914–1918 — Poetry. 3. Soldiers' writings, English. I. Ward, Candace. II. Series.
PR1195.W65W67   1997
821'.912080358 — dc21
                                                96-51566
                                                 CIP

Manufactured in the United States of America
Dover Publications, Inc., 31 East 2nd Street, Mineola, N.Y. 11501

Note

A complex series of treaties, tensions and alliances involving the major and minor European states led to the assassination of Archduke Franz Ferdinand of Austria by Gavrilo Princip, a Serbian nationalist, on June 28, 1914. In response, the armies of Europe were mobilized and by summer's end, the world was at war. But no one could have foreseen the apocolyptic degree of destruction that ensued. By the time the Armistice was signed on November 11, 1918, more than nine million military personnel and five million civilians had been killed. In Great Britain and Europe, an entire generation of young men was wiped out.

Most of the poets in this anthology participated in what came to be called the Great War; many of them did not survive to see its end. Some, like Rupert Brooke and John McCrae, believed their services were part of a noble and just cause. Others — most notably Siegfried Sassoon and Wilfred Owen — entered the military through a sense of duty, though both poets came to see Britain's participation in the war as unnecessarily prolonged. Antiwar sentiment was not uncommon among soldiers, particularly when it became clear that the war was one of attrition. By September 1914, the Allied and Central Powers were locked into trench warfare, and 1915–1916 were years of stalemate characterized by Pyrrhic victories such as that won by the Allies in Champagne, where 500 yards of ground was gained over the course of two months — at a cost of 50,000 men. Such results contributed to a sense of futility experienced by frontline soldiers, and chlorine gas, first deployed on the Western Front on April 22, 1915 at the Battle of Ypres, intensified the horrors of battle. The initial patriotic fervor that compelled many young men to enlist in the summer of 1914 had, in most cases, by 1916 collapsed into cynicism and anger, as reflected in a saying that circulated among the British troops: "Went to war with Rupert Brooke, came home with Siegfried Sassoon."

While not all of the poets contained in this anthology served combat duty, all were touched by the devastation that changed the world's perception of war. Despite the propaganda and intense anti-German sentiment that proliferated during the war, "this was no case," as Edward Thomas wrote, "of petty right or wrong." All of the poetry — whether the manifestation of the poets' despair, outrage or patriotism — stands as a memorial that has outlasted the battlelines of World War One.

Contents

RUPERT BROOKE (1887–1915)

Rupert Brooke, born in 1887, was educated at Rugby School and later at King's College, Cambridge. Perhaps more than any other of the war poets, Brooke came to represent the magnitude of England's sacrifice for what was popularly believed a just cause. Brooke was young, beautiful and gifted; that he wrote poetry justifying the war effort — and that he was killed in the early years of the war — contributed to his myth.

Because he died so young (he was 28 when he died of blood poisoning shortly before the Gallipoli expedition), Brooke's poetry assumed a greater place in English literature than it might have had he lived longer. Prior to the war, he contributed to Edward Marsh's volumes of *Georgian Poetry*, celebrating the English countryside and way of life. He had early on been influenced by the decadent Romanticism of the late nineteenth century, and while at Cambridge, he fell under the influence of the seventeenth-century metaphysical poets. His first volume of poems, *Poems, 1911*, was well received and in 1914 he published *1914 Sonnets*, ensuring his reputation as one of England's rising young poets.

Brooke enlisted shortly after England declared war against Germany on August 4, 1914, and turned his poetic efforts to his experiences as a soldier. The most famous of these was the five-sonnet group comprising *The Soldier*, and in particular the sonnet of the same name. Not long after Brooke wrote the poem, the Dean of St. Paul's cathedral in London read it on Easter Sunday, 1915. It was reprinted in the London *Times* and caused an immediate sensation. The poem's initial reception was magnified by Brooke's own death soon after. His words, "If I should die, think only this of me:/ That there's some corner of a foreign field/ That is forever England," are some of the best remembered of the war's poetry.

I.   PEACE

Now, God be thanked Who has matched us with His hour,
    And caught our youth, and wakened us from sleeping,
With hand made sure, clear eye, and sharpened power,
    To turn, as swimmers into cleanness leaping,

1

Glad from a world grown old and cold and weary,
   Leave the sick hearts that honour could not move,
And half-men, and their dirty songs and dreary,
   And all the little emptiness of love!

Oh! we, who have known shame, we have found release there,
   Where there's no ill, no grief, but sleep has mending,
     Naught broken save this body, lost but breath;
Nothing to shake the laughing heart's long peace there
   But only agony, and that has ending;
     And the worst friend and enemy is but Death.

II.   SAFETY

Dear! of all happy in the hour, most blest
   He who has found our hid security,
Assured in the dark tides of the world that rest,
   And heard our word, 'Who is so safe as we?'
We have found safety with all things undying,
   The winds, and morning, tears of men and mirth,
The deep night, and birds singing, and clouds flying,
   And sleep, and freedom, and the autumnal earth.
We have built a house that is not for Time's throwing.
   We have gained a peace unshaken by pain for ever.
War knows no power. Safe shall be my going,
   Secretly armed against all death's endeavour;
Safe though all safety's lost; safe where men fall;
And if these poor limbs die, safest of all.

III.   THE DEAD

Blow out, you bugles, over the rich Dead!
   There's none of these so lonely and poor of old,
   But, dying, has made us rarer gifts than gold.
These laid the world away; poured out the red
Sweet wine of youth; gave up the years to be
   Of work and joy, and that unhoped serene,
   That men call age; and those who would have been,
Their sons, they gave, their immortality.

Blow, bugles, blow! They brought us, for our dearth,
   Holiness, lacked so long, and Love, and Pain.

Honour has come back, as a king, to earth,
    And paid his subjects with a royal wage;
And Nobleness walks in our ways again;
    And we have come into our heritage.

IV.   THE DEAD

These hearts were woven of human joys and cares,
   Washed marvellously with sorrow, swift to mirth.
The years had given them kindness. Dawn was theirs,
   And sunset, and the colours of the earth.
These had seen movement, and heard music; known
   Slumber and waking; loved; gone proudly friended;
Felt the quick stir of wonder; sat alone;
   Touched flowers and furs and cheeks. All this is ended.

There are waters blown by changing winds to laughter
And lit by the rich skies, all day. And after,
   Frost, with a gesture, stays the waves that dance
And wandering loveliness. He leaves a white
   Unbroken glory, a gathered radiance,
A width, a shining peace, under the night.

☆ V.   THE SOLDIER ☆

If I should die, think only this of me:
   That there's some corner of a foreign field
That is for ever England. There shall be
   In that rich earth a richer dust concealed;
A dust whom England bore, shaped, made aware,
   Gave, once, her flowers to love, her ways to roam,
A body of England's, breathing English air,
   Washed by the rivers, blest by suns of home.

And think, this heart, all evil shed away,
   A pulse in the eternal mind, no less
     Gives somewhere back the thoughts by England given;
Her sights and sounds; dreams happy as her day;
   And laughter, learnt of friends; and gentleness,
     In hearts at peace, under an English heaven.

[Handwritten annotations:]
A B A B C D C D — E F G E F G
sonnet
Petrachan (Italian)
iambic pentameter
formalized form
addressed to members at home
Sonnets are usually love poems — love of country

THE TREASURE

When colour goes home into the eyes,
    And lights that shine are shut again
With dancing girls and sweet birds' cries
    Behind the gateways of the brain;
And that no-place which gave them birth, shall close
The rainbow and the rose: —

Still may Time hold some golden space
    Where I'll unpack that scented store
Of song and flower and sky and face,
    And count, and touch, and turn them o'er,
Musing upon them; as a mother, who
Has watched her children all the rich day through
Sits, quiet-handed, in the fading light,
When children sleep, ere night.

CHARLES HAMILTON SORLEY (1895–1915)

Another poet writing in the early years of the war was Charles Hamilton Sorley. Sorley, the son of middle-class, intellectual parents, attended Marlborough College at Cambridge. From January to July 1914, Sorley traveled in Germany; he had intended to go to Oxford in the autumn of that year, but on August 6, two days after England declared war, he applied for a commission. Despite his early involvement in the war effort, Sorley's was not an unquestioning patriotism, nor did he experience the intense anti-German sentiment pervading England. Indeed, his letters reveal an early and deep skepticism about the war effort, and he was critical of the kind of attitude expressed in Brooke's sonnets. Writing to a friend about "The Soldier," Sorley criticized the self-important stance he read there:

> [Brooke] is far too obsessed with his own sacrifice, regarding the going to war of himself (and others) by the turn of circumstances, where non-compliance with this demand would have made life intolerable. It was not that "they" gave up anything . . . but that the essence of these things had been endangered by circumstances over which he had no control, and he must fight to recapture them. He has clothed his attitude in fine words: but he has taken the sentimental attitude.

The attitude that Sorley exhibited in his own poetry was unsentimental and tragically ironic. Killed at the age of twenty at the Battle of Loos, Sorley saw more actual combat than Brooke, and experienced the horror of the first poison-gas attacks.

TO GERMANY

You are blind like us. Your hurt no man designed,
And no man claimed the conquest of your land.
But gropers both through fields of thought confined
We stumble and we do not understand.
You only saw your future bigly planned,
And we, the tapering paths of our own mind,

And in each other's dearest ways we stand,
And hiss and hate. And the blind fight the blind.

When it is peace, then we may view again
With new-won eyes each other's truer form
And wonder. Grown more loving-kind and warm
We'll grasp firm hands and laugh at the old pain,
When it is peace. But until peace, the storm
The darkness and the thunder and the rain.

'WHEN YOU SEE MILLIONS OF THE MOUTHLESS DEAD'

When you see millions of the mouthless dead
Across your dreams in pale battalions go,
Say not soft things as other men have said,
That you'll remember. For you need not so.
Give them not praise. For, deaf, how should they know
It is not curses heaped on each gashed head?
Nor tears. Their blind eyes see not your tears flow.
Nor honour. It is easy to be dead.
Say only this, 'They are dead.' Then add thereto,
'Yet many a better one has died before.'
Then, scanning all the o'ercrowded mass, should you
Perceive one face that you loved heretofore,
It is a spook. None wears the face you knew.
Great death has made all his for evermore.

ROUTE MARCH

All the hills and vales along
Earth is bursting into song,
And the singers are the chaps
Who are going to die perhaps.
    O sing, marching men,
    Till the valleys ring again.
    Give your gladness to earth's keeping,
    So be glad, when you are sleeping.

Cast away regret and rue,
Think what you are marching to,
Little live, great pass.

Jesus Christ and Barabbas
Were found the same day.
This died, that, went his way.
   So sing with joyful breath.
   For why, you are going to death.
   Teeming earth will surely store
   All the gladness that you pour.

Earth that never doubts nor fears
Earth that knows of death, not tears,
Earth that bore with joyful ease
Hemlock for Socrates,
Earth that blossomed and was glad
'Neath the cross that Christ had,
Shall rejoice and blossom too
When the bullet reaches you.
   Wherefore, men marching
   On the road to death, sing!
   Pour gladness on earth's head,
   So be merry, so be dead.

From the hills and valleys earth
Shouts back the sound of mirth,
Tramp of feet and lilt of song
Ringing all the road along.
All the music of their going,
Ringing swinging glad song-throwing,
Earth will echo still, when foot
Lies numb and voice mute.
   On marching men, on
   To the gates of death with song.
   Sow your gladness for earth's reaping,
   So you may be glad though sleeping.
   Strew your gladness on earth's bed,
   So be merry, so be dead.

EDWARD THOMAS (1878–1917)

Edward Thomas wrote about 150 poems during his literary career, all between 1914 and his death on Easter Monday, 1917. Born in south London, Thomas married at an early age and turned to hack writing to support his family. Only after he became friends with the American poet Robert Frost, who lived in England from 1913 to 1915, did Thomas begin writing verse. Ironically, the war provided Thomas with the impetus to concentrate more fully on his poetic endeavors. He enlisted in July 1915 in the Artists' Rifles and though most of his poems do not refer directly to the war, it provides a context within which to read them. The verse itself tends toward a Georgian appreciation of rural England, though Thomas was not a member of that poetic school. The beauty of the English countryside provided the sharp contrast to the trench warfare in France, which becomes a source of tension in Thomas' verse.

THIS IS NO CASE OF PETTY RIGHT OR WRONG

This is no case of petty right or wrong
That politicians or philosophers
Can judge. I hate not Germans, nor grow hot
With love of Englishmen, to please newspapers.
Beside my hate for one fat patriot
My hatred of the Kaiser is love true: —
A kind of god he is, banging a gong.
But I have not to choose between the two,
Or between justice and injustice. Dinned
With war and argument I read no more
Than in the storm smoking along the wind
Athwart the wood. Two witches' cauldrons roar.
From one the weather shall rise clear and gay;
Out of the other an England beautiful
And like her mother that died yesterday.
Little I know or care if, being dull,

I shall miss something that historians
Can rake out of the ashes when perchance
The phoenix broods serene above their ken.
But with the best and meanest Englishmen
I am one in crying, God save England, lest
We lose what never slaves and cattle blessed.
The ages made her that made us from dust:
She is all we know and live by, and we trust
She is good and must endure, loving her so:
And as we love ourselves we hate our foe.

ADLESTROP

Yes, I remember Adlestrop —
The name, because one afternoon
Of heat the express-train drew up there
Unwontedly. It was late June.

The steam hissed. Someone cleared his throat.
No one left and no one came
On the bare platform. What I saw
Was Adlestrop — only the name

And willows, willow-herb, and grass,
And meadowsweet, and haycocks dry,
No whit less still and lonely fair
Than the high cloudlets in the sky.

And for that minute a blackbird sang
Close by, and round him, mistier,
Farther and farther, all the birds
Of Oxfordshire and Gloucestershire.

TEARS

It seems I have no tears left. They should have fallen —
Their ghosts, if tears have ghosts, did fall — that day
When twenty hounds streamed by me, not yet combed out
But still all equals in their rage of gladness
Upon the scent, made one, like a great dragon
In Blooming Meadow that bends towards the sun
And once bore hops: and on that other day

When I stepped out from the double-shadowed Tower
Into an April morning, stirring and sweet
And warm. Strange solitude was there and silence.
A mightier charm than any in the Tower
Possessed the courtyard. They were changing guard,
Soldiers in line, young English countrymen,
Fair-haired and ruddy, in white tunics. Drums
And fifes were playing 'The British Grenadiers.'
The men, the music piercing that solitude
And silence, told me truths I had not dreamed,
And have forgotten since their beauty passed.

THE OWL

Downhill I came, hungry, and yet not starved;
Cold, yet had heat within me that was proof
Against the North wind; tired, yet so that rest
Had seemed the sweetest thing under a roof.

Then at the inn I had food, fire, and rest,
Knowing how hungry, cold, and tired was I.
All of the night was quite barred out except
An owl's cry, a most melancholy cry

Shaken out long and clear upon the hill,
No merry note, nor cause of merriment,
But one telling me plain what I escaped
And others could not, that night, as in I went.

And salted was my food, and my repose,
Salted and sobered, too, by the bird's voice
Speaking for all who lay under the stars,
Soldiers and poor, unable to rejoice.

A PRIVATE

This plowman dead in battle slept out of doors
Many a frozen night, and merrily
Answered staid drinkers, good bedmen, and all bores:
'At Mrs. Greenland's Hawthorn Bush,' said he,
'I slept.' None knew which bush. Above the town,
Beyond 'The Drover,' a hundred spot the down

In Wiltshire. And where now at last he sleeps
More sound in France — that, too, he secret keeps.

AS THE TEAM'S HEAD BRASS

As the team's head brass flashed out on the turn
The lovers disappeared into the wood.
I sat among the boughs of the fallen elm
That strewed an angle of the fallow, and
Watched the plough narrowing a yellow square
Of charlock. Every time the horses turned
Instead of treading me down, the ploughman leaned
Upon the handles to say or ask a word,
About the weather, next about the war.
Scraping the share he faced towards the wood,
And screwed along the furrow till the brass flashed
Once more.
               The blizzard felled the elm whose crest
I sat in, by a woodpecker's round hole,
The ploughman said. 'When will they take it away?'
'When the war's over.' So the talk began —
One minute and an interval of ten,
A minute more and the same interval.
'Have you been out?' 'No.' 'And don't want to, perhaps?'
'If I could only come back again, I should.
I could spare an arm. I shouldn't want to lose
A leg. If I should lose my head, why, so,
I should want nothing more. . . . Have many gone
From here?' 'Yes.' 'Many lost?' 'Yes, a good few.
Only two teams work on the farm this year.
One of my mates is dead. The second day
In France they killed him. It was back in March,
The very night of the blizzard, too. Now if
He had stayed here we should have moved the tree.'
'And I should not have sat here. Everything
Would have been different. For it would have been
Another world.' 'Ay, and a better, though
If we could see all all might seem good.' Then
The lovers came out of the wood again:
The horses started and for the last time
I watched the clods crumble and topple over
After the ploughshare and the stumbling team.

JOHN McCRAE (1872–1918)

Born in Ontario, Canada, John McCrae was descended from Scottish immigrants. He was educated at the University of Toronto, and in 1898 he received his medical degree. After serving as a medical officer in the Boer War, McCrae returned to Montreal to practice medicine. Soon after World War One began, McCrae returned to military service, traveling to France as a medical officer for the Allied forces. McCrae began publishing poetry during the Boer War, and he was finishing a medical treatise when he left for France. McCrae's most famous — and perhaps only remembered — work is the fifteen-line poem "In Flanders Fields." First published in *Punch* (December 8, 1915), the poem became immediately popular, and was used as a recruiting tool. McCrae died of pneumonia in January 1918, in a hospital in Boulogne.

IN FLANDERS FIELDS

In Flanders fields the poppies blow
Between the crosses, row on row,
That mark our place, and in the sky,
The larks, still bravely singing, fly,
Scarce heard amid the guns below.

We are the dead; short days ago
We lived, felt dawn, saw sunset glow,
Loved and were loved, and now we lie
     In Flanders fields.

Take up our quarrel with the foe!
To you from failing hands we throw
The torch; be yours to hold it high!
If ye break faith with us who die
We shall not sleep, though poppies grow
     In Flanders fields.

ISAAC ROSENBERG (1890–1918)

Unlike most of the war poets in this anthology, Rosenberg did not come from a comfortable middle- or upper-class background, nor was he commissioned as an officer during World War One. The child of a poor Jewish family, Rosenberg grew up in London's East End. He left school at 14, but was a precocious writer and painter; in 1912 he published a small volume of poems entitled *Night and Day*. When the war broke out, Rosenberg was living with an older sister in South Africa. He returned to England in 1915 and enlisted, though not, as he wrote in a letter, "from patriotic reasons." "Nothing," he continued, "can justify war." Like Wilfred Owen, Rosenberg was an innovative poet, and the experiences of his urban youth and during the war, as a private fighting in the trenches, became the raw material that he transformed into much larger and symbolic art. Siegfried Sassoon described Rosenberg's poems as "experiments" exhibiting a "strenuous effort for impassioned expressions." As impassioned as Rosenberg's poetry is, there is also a level of detachment that transcends the brutal realism of the events providing the occasion for the poem.

BREAK OF DAY IN THE TRENCHES

The darkness crumbles away.
It is the same old druid Time as ever,
Only a live thing leaps my hand,
A queer sardonic rat,
As I pull the parapet's poppy
To stick behind my ear.
Droll rat, they would shoot you if they knew
Your cosmopolitan sympathies.
Now you have touched this English hand
You will do the same to a German
Soon, no doubt, if it be your pleasure
To cross the sleeping green between.
It seems you inwardly grin as you pass

13

Strong eyes, fine limbs, haughty athletes,
Less chanced than you for life,
Bonds to the whims of murder,
Sprawled in the bowels of the earth,
The torn fields of France.
What do you see in our eyes
At the shrieking iron and flame
Hurled through still heavens?
What quaver — what heart aghast?
Poppies whose roots are in man's veins
Drop, and are ever dropping;
But mine in my ear is safe —
Just a little white with the dust.

LOUSE HUNTING

Nudes — stark and glistening,
Yelling in lurid glee. Grinning faces
And raging limbs
Whirl over the floor one fire.
For a shirt verminously busy
Yon soldier tore from his throat, with oaths
Godhead might shrink at, but not the lice.
And soon the shirt was aflare
Over the candle he'd lit while we lay.

Then we all sprang up and stript
To hunt the verminous brood.
Soon like a demons' pantomime
The place was raging.
See the silhouettes agape,
See the gibbering shadows
Mixed with the battled arms on the wall.
See gargantuan hooked fingers
Pluck in supreme flesh
To smutch supreme littleness.
See the merry limbs in hot Highland fling
Because some wizard vermin
Charmed from the quiet this revel
When our ears were half lulled
By the dark music
Blown from Sleep's trumpet.

RETURNING, WE HEAR THE LARKS

Sombre the night is.
And though we have our lives, we know
What sinister threat lurks there.

Dragging these anguished limbs, we only know
This poison-blasted track opens on our camp —
On a little safe sleep.

But hark! joy — joy — strange joy.
Lo! heights of night ringing with unseen larks.
Music showering on our upturned list'ning faces.

Death could drop from the dark
As easily as song —
But song only dropped,
Like a blind man's dreams on the sand
By dangerous tides,
Like a girl's dark hair for she dreams no ruin lies there,
Or her kisses where a serpent hides.

DEAD MAN'S DUMP

The plunging limbers over the shattered track
Racketed with their rusty freight,
Stuck out like many crowns of thorns,
And the rusty stakes like sceptres old
To stay the flood of brutish men
Upon our brothers dear.

The wheels lurched over sprawled dead
But pained them not, though their bones crunched,
Their shut mouths made no moan.
They lie there huddled, friend and foeman,
Man born of man, and born of woman,
And shells go crying over them
From night till night and now.

Earth has waited for them,
All the time of their growth
Fretting for their decay:

Now she has them at last!
In the strength of their strength
Suspended — stopped and held.

What fierce imaginings their dark souls lit?
Earth! have they gone into you?
Somewhere they must have gone,
And flung on your hard back
Is their soul's sack,
Emptied of God-ancestralled essences.
Who hurled them out? Who hurled?

None saw their spirits' shadow shake the grass,
Or stood aside for the half-used life to pass
Out of those doomed nostrils and the doomed mouth,
When the swift iron burning bee
Drained the wild honey of their youth.

What of us who, flung on the shrieking pyre,
Walk, our usual thoughts untouched,
Our lucky limbs as on ichor fed,
Immortal seeming ever?
Perhaps when the flames beat loud on us,
A fear may choke in our veins
And the startled blood may stop.

The air is loud with death,
The dark air spurts with fire,
The explosions ceaseless are.
Timelessly now, some minutes past,
These dead strode time with vigorous life,
Till the shrapnel called 'An end!'
But not to all. In bleeding pangs
Some borne on stretchers dreamed of home,
Dear things, war-blotted from their hearts.

A man's brains splattered on
A stretcher-bearer's face;
His shook shoulders slipped their load,
But when they bent to look again
The drowning soul was sunk too deep
For human tenderness.

They left this dead with the older dead,
Stretched at the crossroads.

Burnt black by strange decay
Their sinister faces lie;
The lid over each eye,
The grass and coloured clay
More motion have than they,
Joined to the great sunk silences.

Here is one not long dead;
His dark hearing caught our far wheels,
And the choked soul stretched weak hands
To reach the living word the far wheels said,
The blood-dazed intelligence beating for light,
Crying through the suspense of the far torturing wheels
Swift for the end to break,
Or the wheels to break,
Cried as the tide of the world broke over his sight.

Will they come? Will they ever come?
Even as the mixed hoofs of the mules,
The quivering-bellied mules,
And the rushing wheels all mixed
With his tortured upturned sight.
So we crashed round the bend,
We heard his weak scream,
We heard his very last sound,
And our wheels grazed his dead face.

WILFRED OWEN (1893–1918)

Wilfred Owen is perhaps the most technically innovative and most influential of the World War One poets. Unlike most of the poets in this collection, Owen did not receive a university education. After attending Shrewsbury Technical School until he was 17, he became a lay reader for a minister, but soon left that position to travel to France. From 1913 to 1915, he worked as a private tutor and began writing poetry. Owen returned to England in the summer of 1915 and enlisted in the Artists' Rifles regiment. In 1917 he was wounded three times, and finally sent to England, diagnosed as a victim of shell shock. He met Siegfried Sassoon in the summer of 1917 and the two developed a close relationship. Though Sassoon provided Owen with literary guidance and advice, Owen's poetry differs from Sassoon's epigrammatic style. "My subject is war," Owen wrote of his work, "and the pity of war. The Poetry is in the pity. Yet these elegies are to this generation in no sense consolatory. They may be to the next. All the poet can do is to warn. That is why true poets must be truthful." Owen's poetic skills were honed by the nature of his war experiences and, had he survived the war, he might, as some critics have speculated, vied with T. S. Eliot as the arbiter of poetic taste in the postwar years. As it happened, Owen was killed in action on November 4, 1918, only days before the Armistice was signed. Owen's death, so close to the end of a war he so strenuously objected to, adds a poignancy to the poems that were published posthumously in 1920, collected and introduced by Sassoon.

ARMS AND THE BOY

Let the boy try along this bayonet-blade
How cold steel is, and keen with hunger of blood;
Blue with all malice, like a madman's flash;
And thinly drawn with famishing for flesh.

Lend him to stroke these blind, blunt bullet-leads
Which long to nuzzle in the hearts of lads,

Or give him cartridges of fine zinc teeth,
Sharp with the sharpness of grief and death.

For his teeth seem for laughing round an apple.
There lurk no claws behind his fingers supple;
And God will grow no talons at his heels,
Nor antlers through the thickness of his curls.

GREATER LOVE

Red lips are not so red
    As the stained stones kissed by the English dead.
Kindness of wooed and wooer
Seems shame to their love pure.
O Love, your eyes lose lure
    When I behold eyes blinded in my stead!

Your slender attitude
    Trembles not exquisite like limbs knife-skewed,
Rolling and rolling there
Where God seems not to care;
Till the fierce love they bear
    Cramps them in death's extreme decrepitude.

Your voice sings not so soft, —
    Though even as wind murmuring through raftered loft, —
Your dear voice is not dear,
Gentle, and evening clear,
As theirs whom none now hear,
    Now earth has stopped their piteous mouths that coughed.

Heart, you were never hot
    Nor large, nor full like hearts made great with shot;
And though your hand be pale,
Paler are all which trail
Your cross through flame and hail:
    Weep, you may weep, for you may touch them not.

INSENSIBILITY

1

Happy are men who yet before they are killed
Can let their veins run cold.
Whom no compassion fleers
Or makes their feet
Sore on the alleys cobbled with their brothers.
The front line withers,
But they are troops who fade, not flowers
For poets' tearful fooling:
Men, gaps for filling:
Losses who might have fought
Longer; but no one bothers.

2

And some cease feeling
Even themselves or for themselves.
Dullness best solves
The tease and doubt of shelling,
And Chance's strange arithmetic
Comes simpler than the reckoning of their shilling.
They keep no check on armies' decimation.

3

Happy are these who lose imagination:
They have enough to carry with ammunition.
Their spirit drags no pack,
Their old wounds save with cold cannot more ache.
Having seen all things red,
Their eyes are rid
Of the hurt of the colour of blood for ever.
And terror's first constriction over,
Their senses in some scorching cautery of battle
Now long since ironed,
Can laugh among the dying, unconcerned.

4

Happy the soldier home, with not a notion
How somewhere, every dawn, some men attack,
And many sighs are drained.
Happy the lad whose mind was never trained:

His days are worth forgetting more than not.
He sings along the march
Which we march taciturn, because of dusk,
The long, forlorn, relentless trend
From larger day to huger night.

5

We wise, who with a thought besmirch
Blood over all our soul,
How should we seek our task
But through his blunt and lashless eyes?
Alive, he is not vital overmuch;
Dying, not mortal overmuch;
Nor sad, nor proud,
Nor curious at all.
He cannot tell
Old men's placidity from his.

6

But cursed are dullards whom no cannon stuns,
That they should be as stones;
Wretched are they, and mean
With paucity that never was simplicity.
By choice they made themselves immune
To pity and whatever mourns in man
Before the last sea and the hapless stars;
Whatever mourns when many leave these shores;
Whatever shares
The eternal reciprocity of tears.

DULCE ET DECORUM EST

Bent double, like old beggars under sacks,
Knock-kneed, coughing like hags, we cursed through sludge,
Till on the haunting flares we turned our backs,
And towards our distant rest began to trudge.
Men marched asleep. Many had lost their boots
But limped on, blood-shod. All went lame; all blind;
Drunk with fatigue; deaf even to the hoots
Of tired, outstripped Five-Nines that dropped behind.

Gas! Gas! Quick, boys! — An ecstasy of fumbling,
Fitting the clumsy helmets just in time,

But someone still was yelling out and stumbling
And flound'ring like a man in fire or lime . . .
Dim through the misty panes and thick green light,
As under a green sea, I saw him drowning.

In all my dreams before my helpless sight,
He plunges at me, guttering, choking, drowning.

If in some smothering dreams you too could pace
Behind the wagon that we flung him in,
And watch the white eyes writhing in his face,
His hanging face, like a devil's sick of sin,
If you could hear, at every jolt, the blood
Come gargling from the froth-corrupted lungs
Obscene as cancer, bitter as the cud
Of vile, incurable sores on innocent tongues, —
My friend, you would not tell with such high zest
To children ardent for some desperate glory,
The old lie: *Dulce et decorum est
Pro patria mori*.[1]

☙ MENTAL CASES

Who are these? Why sit they here in twilight?
Wherefore rock they, purgatorial shadows,
Drooping tongues from jaws that slob their relish,
Baring teeth that leer like skulls' teeth wicked?
Stroke on stroke of pain, — but what slow panic,
Gouged these chasms round their fretted sockets?
Ever from their hair and through their hands' palms
Misery swelters. Surely we have perished
Sleeping, and walk hell; but who these hellish?

— These are men whose minds the Dead have ravished.
Memory fingers in their hair of murders,
Multitudinous murders they once witnessed.
Wading sloughs of flesh these helpless wander,
Treading blood from lungs that had loved laughter.
Always they must see these things and hear them,
Batter of guns and shatter of flying muscles,

---

[1] *Dulce . . . mori*] It is a sweet and fitting thing to die for your country.

Carnage incomparable, and human squander
Rucked too thick for these men's extrication.
Therefore still their eyeballs shrink tormented
Back into their brains, because on their sense
Sunlight seems a blood-smear; night comes blood-black;
Dawn breaks open like a wound that bleeds afresh.
— Thus their heads wear this hilarious, hideous,
Awful falseness of set-smiling corpses.
— Thus their hands are plucking at each other;
Picking at the rope-knouts of their scourging;
Snatching after us who smote them, brother,
Pawing us who dealt them war and madness.

FUTILITY

Move him into the sun —
Gently its touch awoke him once,
At home, whispering of fields unsown.
Always it woke him, even in France,
Until this morning and this snow.
If anything might rouse him now
The kind old sun will know.

Think how it wakes the seeds —
Woke, once, the clays of a cold star.
Are limbs, so dear-achieved, are sides
Full-nerved, — still warm, — too hard to stir?
Was it for this the clay grew tall?
— Oh, what made fatuous sunbeams toil
To break earth's sleep at all?

DISABLED

He sat in a wheeled chair, waiting for dark,
And shivered in his ghastly suit of gray,
Legless, sewn short at elbow. Through the park
Voices of boys rang saddening like a hymn,
Voices of play and pleasures after day,
    Till gathering sleep had mothered them from him.

*   *   *

About this time Town used to swing so gay
When glow-lamps budded in the light blue trees,

And girls glanced lovelier as the air grew dim, —
In the old times, before he threw away his knees.
Now he will never feel again how slim
Girls' waists are, or how warm their subtle hands;
All of them touch him like some queer disease.

         *   *   *

There was an artist silly for his face,
For it was younger than his youth, last year.
Now, he is old; his back will never brace;
He's lost his colour very far from here,
Poured it down shell-holes till the veins ran dry,
And half his lifetime lapsed in the hot race,
And leap of purple spurted from his thigh.

         *   *   *

One time he liked a blood-smear down his leg,
After the matches, carried shoulder high.
It was after football, when he'd drunk a peg,
He thought he'd better join. — He wonders why.
Someone had said he'd look a god in kilts,
That's why; and may be, too, to please his Meg;
Aye, that was it, to please the giddy jilts
He asked to join. He didn't have to beg;
Smiling they wrote his lie; aged nineteen years.
Germans he scarcely thought of; all their guilt,
And Austria's, did not move him. And no fears
Of Fear came yet. He thought of jewelled hilts
For daggers in plaid socks; of smart salutes;
And care of arms; and leave; and pay arrears;
Esprit de corps; and hints for young recruits.
And soon he was drafted out with drums and cheers.

         *   *   *

Some cheered him home, but not as crowds cheer Goal.
Only a solemn man who brought him fruits
Thanked him; and then inquired about his soul.

         *   *   *

Now, he will spend a few sick years in Institutes,
And do what things the rules consider wise,
And take whatever pity they may dole.
To-night he noticed how the women's eyes
Passed from him to the strong men that were whole.

How cold and late it is! Why don't they come
And put him into bed? Why don't they come?

🖋 ANTHEM FOR DOOMED YOUTH

What passing-bells for these who die as cattle?
    Only the monstrous anger of the guns.
Only the stuttering rifles' rapid rattle
    Can patter out their hasty orisons.
No mockeries now for them; no prayers nor bells,
    Nor any voice of mourning save the choirs, —
The shrill, demented choirs of wailing shells;
    And bugles calling for them from sad shires.

What candles may be held to speed them all?
    Not in the hands of boys, but in their eyes
Shall shine the holy glimmers of good-byes.
    The pallor of girls' brows shall be their pall;
Their flowers the tenderness of patient minds,
And each slow dusk a drawing-down of blinds.

🖋   STRANGE MEETING

It seemed that out of battle I escaped
Down some profound dull tunnel, long since scooped
Through granites which titanic wars had groined.
Yet also there encumbered sleepers groaned,
Too fast in thought or death to be bestirred.
Then, as I probed them, one sprang up, and stared
With piteous recognition in fixed eyes,
Lifting distressful hands as if to bless.
And by his smile, I knew that sullen hall,
By his dead smile I knew we stood in Hell.
With a thousand pains that vision's face was grained;
Yet no blood reached there from the upper ground,
And no guns thumped, or down the flues made moan.
'Strange friend,' I said, 'here is no cause to mourn.'
'None,' said that other, 'save the undone years,
The hopelessness. Whatever hope is yours,
Was my life also; I went hunting wild
After the wildest beauty in the world,
Which lies not calm in eyes, or braided hair,
But mocks the steady running of the hour,

And if it grieves, grieves richlier than here.
For of my glee might many men have laughed,
And of my weeping something had been left,
Which must die now. I mean the truth untold,
The pity of war, the pity war distilled.
Now men will go content with what we spoiled.
Or, discontent, boil bloody, and be spilled.
They will be swift with swiftness of the tigress,
None will break ranks, though nations trek from progress.
Courage was mine, and I had mystery,
Wisdom was mine, and I had mastery:
To miss the march of this retreating world
Into vain citadels that are not walled.
Then, when much blood had clogged their chariot-wheels
I would go up and wash them from sweet wells,
Even with truths that lie too deep for taint.
I would have poured my spirit without stint
But not through wounds; not on the cess of war.
Foreheads of men have bled where no wounds were.
I am the enemy you killed, my friend.
I knew you in this dark; for so you frowned
Yesterday through me as you jabbed and killed.
I parried; but my hands were loath and cold.
Let us sleep now. . . .'

APOLOGIA PRO POEMATE MEO[1]

I, too, saw God through mud, —
    The mud that cracked on cheeks when wretches smiled.
    War brought more glory to their eyes than blood,
    And gave their laughs more glee than shakes a child.

Merry it was to laugh there —
    Where death becomes absurd and life absurder.
    For power was on us as we slashed bones bare
    Not to feel sickness or remorse of murder.

[1] *Apologia . . . meo*] Apology for my poem.

I, too, have dropped off Fear —
    Behind the barrage, dead as my platoon,
    And sailed my spirit surging light and clear
    Past the entanglement where hopes lay strewn;

And witnessed exultation —
    Faces that used to curse me, scowl for scowl,
    Shine and lift up with passion of oblation,
    Seraphic for an hour; though they were foul.

I have made fellowships —
    Untold of happy lovers in old song.
    For love is not the binding of fair lips
    With the soft silk of eyes that look and long,

By Joy, whose ribbon slips, —
    But wound with war's hard wire whose stakes are strong;
    Bound with the bandage of the arm that drips;
    Knit in the webbing of the rifle-thong.

I have perceived much beauty
    In the hoarse oaths that kept our courage straight;
    Heard music in the silentness of duty;
    Found peace where shell-storms spouted reddest spate.

Nevertheless, except you share
    With them in hell the sorrowful dark of hell,
    Whose world is but the trembling of a flare
    And heaven but as the highway for a shell,

You shall not hear their mirth:
    You shall not come to think them well content
    By any jest of mine. These men are worth
    Your tears. You are not worth their merriment.

IVOR GURNEY (1890–1937)

Ivor Gurney was born in Gloucester, to a lower-middle-class professional family. Early on he showed musical talent, and with the help of a local patron, was awarded a scholarship to the Royal College of Music. When the war broke out, Gurney enlisted, but was turned down because of poor eyesight. He was accepted when he enlisted again in 1915, and was sent to France in 1916. Gurney was acutely sensitive to the horrors of the war, and after being wounded in April and gassed in August of 1917, he was sent to a mental hospital. Gurney's mental health had always been precarious, and his war experiences exacerbated his condition. Though there were periods of recovery from the paranoid schizophrenia from which he suffered, Gurney was finally confined to a mental home in Gloucester in 1922, and later to the City of London Mental Hospital in Kent, where he remained until his death in 1937. During his lifetime Gurney achieved a modest fame as a composer, his music heavily influenced by poetry. He created song cycles to the works of A. E. Housman and that of his fellow war poet Edward Thomas, as well as to the poems of John Clare, the nineteenth-century poet whose verse Gurney set to music while confined in the mental asylum. Gerard Manley Hopkins provided another poetic inspiration for Gurney, and in his poems as well as music, one can trace the same tensions of melancholy and despair that characterize much of Hopkins' poetry.

THE SILENT ONE

Who died on the wires, and hung there, one of two —
Who for his hours of life had chattered through
Infinite lovely chatter of Bucks accent:
Yet faced unbroken wires; stepped over, and went
A noble fool, faithful to his stripes — and ended.
But I weak, hungry, and willing only for the chance
Of line — to fight in the line, lay down under unbroken
Wires, and saw the flashes and kept unshaken,
Till the politest voice — a finicking accent, said:

'Do you think you might crawl through, there: there's a hole'
Darkness, shot at: I smiled, as politely replied —
'I'm afraid not, Sir.' There was no hole no way to be seen
Nothing but chance of death, after tearing of clothes
Kept flat, and watched the darkness, hearing bullets whizzing —
And thought of music — and swore deep heart's deep oaths
(Polite to God) and retreated and came on again,
Again retreated — and a second time faced the screen.

TO HIS LOVE

He's gone, and all our plans
        Are useless indeed.
We'll walk no more on Cotswold
        Where the sheep feed
        Quietly and take no heed.

His body that was so quick
        Is not as you
Knew it, on Severn river
        Under the blue
        Driving our small boat through.

You would not know him now . . .
        But still he died
Nobly, so cover him over
        With violets of pride
        Purple from Severn side.

Cover him, cover him soon!
        And with thick-set
Masses of memoried flowers —
        Hide that red wet
        Thing I must somehow forget.

THE TARGET

I shot him, and it had to be
One of us! 'Twas him or me.
'Couldn't be helped,' and none can blame
Me, for you would do the same.

My mother, she can't sleep for fear
Of what might be a-happening here
To me. Perhaps it might be best
To die, and set her fears at rest.

For worst is worst, and worry's done.
Perhaps he was the only son . . .
Yet God keeps still, and does not say
A word of guidance any way.

Well, if they get me, first I'll find
That boy, and tell him all my mind,
And see who felt the bullet worst,
And ask his pardon, if I durst.

All's a tangle. Here's my job.
A man might rave, or shout, or sob;
And God He takes no sort of heed.
This is a bloody mess indeed.

SIEGFRIED SASSOON (1886–1967)

The war poems of Siegfried Sassoon are biting satires condemning the war. Describing such poems as "The One-Legged Man" as "satirical drawings," Sassoon acknowledged that he intended to "disturb complacency" with his art. Sassoon himself served valiantly in the war's early years, and was awarded the Military Cross for bravery. But as the war continued, Sassoon came to the conclusion that it was being needlessly prolonged. In the summer of 1917, he submitted his now famous protest against the war to his commanding officer, which was reprinted in the press. In it Sassoon declared that he had entered the war believing it was one of "defence and liberation"; but he now saw it as a war of "aggression and conquest"; he could "no longer be a party to prolong these sufferings for ends which I believe evil and unjust." Incendiary as Sassoon's statement was, its impact was lessened through the efforts of his friend and fellow poet Robert Graves, who used his influence to protect Sassoon. Rather than having to face a court martial, Sassoon was tried by a medical board and judged to be suffering from severe shell shock. Sassoon's account of the investigation appears in the autobiographical *Memoirs of an Infantry Officer* (1931). After the medical board's ruling, Sassoon was sent to Craiglockhart military hospital (where he met Wilfred Owen), and while there composed some of his finest war poems. Sassoon published his first volume of war poetry, *The Old Huntsman*, in May 1917, and a second volume, *Counter-Attack*, in July 1918. Perhaps the greatest irony of Sassoon's poetry was its popular success. As Bernard Bergonzi observes, "Sassoon's anti-war outcry had been transformed . . . into a subtler form of pro-war propaganda," and some of the very people he condemned — politicians and civilians alike — celebrated his verse.

'IN THE PINK'

So Davies wrote: 'This leaves me in the pink.'
Then scrawled his name: 'Your loving sweetheart, Willie.'
With crosses for a hug. He'd had a drink
Of rum and tea; and, though the barn was chilly,

For once his blood ran warm; he had pay to spend.
Winter was passing; soon the year would mend.

He couldn't sleep that night. Stiff in the dark
He groaned and thought of Sundays at the farm,
When he'd go out as cheerful as a lark
In his best suit to wander arm-in-arm
With brown-eyed Gwen, and whisper in her ear
The simple, silly things she liked to hear.

And then he thought: tomorrow night we trudge
Up to the trenches, and my boots are rotten.
Five miles of stodgy clay and freezing sludge,
And everything but wretchedness forgotten.
Tonight he's in the pink; but soon he'll die.
And still the war goes on; *he* don't know why.

A WORKING PARTY

Three hours ago he blundered up the trench,
Sliding and poising, groping with his boots;
Sometimes he tripped and lurched against the walls
With hands that pawed the sodden bags of chalk.
He couldn't see the man who walked in front;
Only he heard the drum and rattle of feet
Stepping along the trench-boards, — often splashing
Wretchedly where the sludge was ankle-deep.

Voices would grunt, 'Keep to your right, — make way!'
When squeezing past the men from the front-line:
White faces peered, puffing a point of red;
Candles and braziers glinted through the chinks
And curtain-flaps of dug-outs; then the gloom
Swallowed his sense of sight; he stooped and swore
Because a sagging wire had caught his neck.
A flare went up; the shining whiteness spread
And flickered upward, showing nimble rats,
And mounds of glimmering sand-bags, bleached with rain;
Then the slow, silver moment died in dark.
The wind came posting by with chilly gusts
And buffeting at corners, piping thin
And dreary through the crannies; rifle-shots

Would split and crack and sing along the night,
And shells came calmly through the drizzling air
To burst with hollow bang below the hill.

Three hours ago he stumbled up the trench;
Now he will never walk that road again:
He must be carried back, a jolting lump
Beyond all need of tenderness and care;
A nine-stone corpse with nothing more to do.

He was a young man with a meagre wife
And two pale children in a Midland town;
He showed the photograph to all his mates;
And they considered him a decent chap
Who did his work and hadn't much to say,
And always laughed at other people's jokes
Because he hadn't any of his own.

That night when he was busy at his job
Of piling bags along the parapet,
He thought how slow time went, stamping his feet,
And blowing on his fingers, pinched with cold.
He thought of getting back by half-past twelve,
And tot of rum to send him warm to sleep
In draughty dug-out frowsty with the fumes
Of coke, and full of snoring, weary men.

He pushed another bag along the top,
Craning his body outward; then a flare
Gave one white glimpse of No Man's Land and wire;
And as he dropped his head the instant split
His startled life with lead, and all went out.

'BLIGHTERS'

The House is crammed: tier beyond tier they grin
And cackle at the Show, while prancing ranks
Of harlots shrill the chorus, drunk with din;
'We're sure the Kaiser loves the dear old Tanks!'

I'd like to see a Tank come down the stalls,
Lurching to ragtime tunes, or 'Home, Sweet Home,' —

And there'd be no more jokes in Music-halls
To mock the riddled corpses round Bapaume.

handwritten notes: anglican church officer class — Bishop changed for better · Soldiers ran breed an honorable war. · soldier say no that is not the case — bodies + race regressing.

'THEY'

The Bishop tells us: 'When the boys come back
They will not be the same; for they'll have fought
In a just cause: they lead the last attack
On Anti-Christ; their comrade's blood has bought
New right to breed an honorable race.
They have challenged Death and dared him face to face.'

'We're none of us the same!' the boys reply.
'For George lost both his legs; and Bill's stone blind;
Poor Jim's shot through the lungs and like to die;
And Bert's gone syphilitic: you'll not find
A chap who's served that hasn't found *some* change.'
And the bishop said: 'The ways of God are strange!'

handwritten margin note: Cernons

THE ONE-LEGGED MAN

Propped on a stick he viewed the August weald;
Squat orchard trees and oasts with painted cowls;
A homely, tangled hedge, a corn-stooked field,
With sound of barking dogs and farmyard fowls.

And he'd come home again to find it more
Desirable than ever it was before.
How right it seemed that he should reach the span
Of comfortable years allowed to man!
Splendid to eat and sleep and choose a wife,
Safe with his wound, a citizen of life.
He hobbled blithely through the garden gate,
And thought: 'Thank God they had to amputate!'

handwritten margin note: rather be an amputee than face other punishment or battlefield.

HAUNTED

Evening was in the wood, louring with storm.
A time of drought had sucked the weedy pool
And baked the channels; birds had done with song.
Thirst was a dream of fountains in the moon,

Or willow-music blown across the water
Leisurely sliding on by weir and mill.

Uneasy was the man who wandered, brooding,
His face a little whiter than the dusk.
A drone of sultry wings flicker'd in his head.

The end of sunset burning thro' the boughs
Died in a smear of red; exhausted hours
Cumber'd, and ugly sorrows hemmed him in.

He thought: 'Somewhere there's thunder,' as he strove
To shake off dread; he dared not look behind him,
But stood, the sweat of horror on his face.

He blundered down a path, trampling on thistles,
In sudden race to leave the ghostly trees.
And: 'Soon I'll be in open fields,' he thought,
And half-remembered starlight on the meadows,
Scent of mown grass and voices of tired men,
Fading along the field-paths; home and sleep
And cool-swept upland spaces, whispering leaves,
And far off the long churring night-jar's note.

But something in the wood, trying to daunt him,
Led him confused in circles through the brake.
He was forgetting his old wretched folly,
And freedom was his need; his throat was choking;
Barbed brambles gripped and clawed him round his legs,
And he floundered over snags and hidden stumps.
Mumbling: 'I will get out! I must get out!'
Butting and thrusting up the baffling gloom,
Pausing to listen in a space 'twixt thorns,
He peers around with boding, frantic eyes.
An evil creature in the twilight looping,
Flapped blindly in his face. Beating it off,
He screeched in terror, and straightway something clambered
Heavily from an oak, and dropped, bent double,
To shamble at him zigzag, squat and bestial.

Headlong he charges down the wood, and falls
With roaring brain — agony — the snap't spark —

And blots of green and purple in his eyes.
Then the slow fingers groping on his neck,
And at his heart the strangling clasp of death.

THE TROOPS

Dim, gradual thinning of the shapeless gloom
Shudders to drizzling daybreak that reveals
Disconsolate men who stamp their sodden boots
And turn dulled, sunken faces to the sky
Haggard and hopeless. They, who have beaten down
The stale despair of night, must now renew
Their desolation in the truce of dawn,
Murdering the livid hours that grope for peace.

Yet these, who cling to life with stubborn hands,
Can grin through storms of death and find a gap
In the clawed, cruel tangles of his defence.
They march from safety, and the bird-sung joy
Of grass-green thickets, to the land where all
Is ruin, and nothing blossoms but the sky
That hastens over them where they endure
Sad, smoking, flat horizons, reeking woods,
And foundered trench-lines volleying doom for doom.

O my brave brown companions, when your souls
Flock silently away, and the eyeless dead
Shame the wild beast of battle on the ridge,
Death will stand grieving in that field of war
Since your unvanquished hardihood is spent.
And through some mooned Valhalla there will pass
Battalions and battalions, scarred from hell;
The unreturning army that was youth;
The legions who have suffered and are dust.

THE GENERAL

'Good-morning; good-morning!' the General said
When we met him last week on our way to the line.
Now the soldiers he smiled at are most of 'em dead,
And we're cursing his staff for incompetent swine.

'He's a cheery old card,' grunted Harry to Jack
As they slogged up to Arras with rifle and pack.

* * *

But he did for them both by his plan of attack.

REPRESSION OF WAR EXPERIENCE

[handwritten: Shell shock]
[handwritten: paternal Strving]

Now light the candles; one; two; there's a moth;
What silly beggars they are to blunder in
And scorch their wings with glory, liquid flame —
No, no, not that, — it's bad to think of war,
When thoughts you've gagged all day come back to scare you;
And it's been proved that soldiers don't go mad
Unless they lose control of ugly thoughts
That drive them out to jabber among the trees.

Now light your pipe; look, what a steady hand.
Draw a deep breath; stop thinking, count fifteen,
And you're as right as rain. . . .

[handwritten: calm oneself]

                              Why won't it rain?
I wish there'd be a thunder-storm tonight,
With bucketsful of water to sluice the dark,
And make the roses hang their dripping heads.
Books; what a jolly company they are,
Standing so quiet and patient on their shelves,
Dressed in dim brown, and black, and white, and green,
And every kind of colour. Which will you read?
Come on; O *do* read something; they're so wise.
I tell you all the wisdom of the world
Is waiting for you on those shelves; and yet
You sit and gnaw your nails, and let your pipe out,
And listen to the silence: on the ceiling
There's one big, dizzy moth that bumps and flutters;
And in the breathless air outside the house
The garden waits for something that delays.
There must be crowds of ghosts among the trees, —
Not people killed in battle, — they're in France, —
But horrible shapes in shrouds — old men who died
Slow, natural deaths, — old men with ugly souls,
Who wore their bodies out with nasty sins.

* * *

Still
living
how
political
message

You're quiet and peaceful, summering safe at home;
You'd never think there was a bloody war on! . . .
O yes, you would . . . why, you can hear the guns.
Hark! Thud, thud, thud, — quite soft . . . they never cease —
Those whispering guns — O Christ, I want to go out
And screech at them to stop — I'm going crazy;
I'm going stark, staring mad because of the guns.

TRENCH DUTY

Shaken from sleep, and numbed and scarce awake,
Out in the trench with three hours' watch to take,
I blunder through the splashing mirk; and then
Hear the gruff muttering voices of the men
Crouching in cabins candle-chinked with light.
Hark! There's the big bombardment on our right
Rumbling and bumping; and the dark's a glare
Of flickering horror in the sectors where
We raid the Boche; men waiting, stiff and chilled,
Or crawling on their bellies through the wire.
'What? Stretcher-bearers wanted? Some one killed?'
Five minutes ago I heard a sniper fire:
Why did he do it? . . . Starlight overhead —
Blank stars. I'm wide-awake; and some chap's dead.

PICTURE-SHOW

And still they come and go: and this is all I know —
That from the gloom I watch an endless picture-show,
Where wild or listless faces flicker on their way,
With glad or grievous hearts I'll never understand
Because Time spins so fast, and they've no time to stay
Beyond the moment's gesture of a lifted hand.

And still, between the shadow and the blinding flame,
The brave despair of men flings onward, ever the same
As in those doom-lit years that wait them, and have been . . .
And life is just the picture dancing on a screen.

ROBERT GRAVES (1895–1985)

Robert Graves was born in Wimbledon. Immediately after finishing studies at the public school of Charterhouse, he enlisted in the Army. As a member of the Royal Welch Fusiliers, Graves participated in some of the most brutal battles of the war, including the Battle of Loos, in which Charles Sorley was killed. From these experiences Graves compiled two volumes of war poetry, *Over the Brazier* (1916) and *Fairies and Fusiliers* (1917). The work of a young poet, many of these poems are powerful statements, though Graves himself was highly critical of them: in his *Collected Poems* (1914–47), Graves omitted all of the war poems except for the retrospective "Recalling War," which was written twenty years after the war. Not until his autobiography, *Goodbye to All That* (1929, 1957), did Graves come to terms with his war experiences. But in the poetry itself, one can get an idea of the tension between the Georgian poetics of his schooldays and the brutality of trench warfare.

TO LUCASTA ON GOING TO THE WAR — FOR THE FOURTH TIME

It doesn't matter what's the cause,
    What wrong they say we're righting,
A curse for treaties, bonds and laws,
    When we're to do the fighting!
And since we lads are proud and true,
    What else remains to do?
Lucasta, when to France your man
Returns his fourth time, hating war,
Yet laughs as calmly as he can
    And flings an oath, but says no more,
That is not courage, that's not fear —
Lucasta he's a Fusilier,
    And his pride sends him here.

Let statesmen bluster, bark and bray,
  And so decide who started
This bloody war, and who's to pay,
  But he must be stout-hearted,
Must sit and stake with quiet breath,
  Playing at cards with Death.
Don't plume yourself he fights for you;
It is no courage, love, or hate,
But let us do the things we do;
  It's pride that makes the heart be great;
It is not anger, no, nor fear —
Lucasta he's a Fusilier,
  And his pride keeps him here.

GOLIATH AND DAVID

(For D. C. T., killed at Fricourt, March, 1916)

Yet once an earlier David took
Smooth pebbles from the brook:
Out between the lines he went
To that one-sided tournament,
A shepherd boy who stood out fine
And young to fight a Philistine
Clad all in brazen mail. He swears
That he's killed lions, he's killed bears,
And those that scorn the God of Zion
Shall perish so like bear or lion.
But . . . the historian of that fight
Had not the heart to tell it right.

Striding within javelin range,
Goliath marvels at this strange
Goodly-faced boy so proud of strength.
David's clear eye measures the length;
With hand thrust back, he cramps one knee,
Poises a moment thoughtfully,
And hurls with a long vengeful swing.
The pebble, humming from the sling
Like a wild bee, flies a sure line
For the forehead of the Philistine;

Then . . . but there comes a brazen clink,
And quicker than a man can think
Goliath's shield parries each cast.
Clang! clang! and clang! was David's last.
Scorn blazes in the Giant's eye,
Towering unhurt six cubits high.
Says foolish David, 'Damn your shield!
And damn my sling! but I'll not yield.'
He takes his staff of Mamre oak,
A knotted shepherd-staff that's broke
The skull of many a wolf and fox
Come filching lambs from Jesse's flocks.
Loud laughs Goliath, and that laugh
Can scatter chariots like blown chaff
To rout; but David, calm and brave,
Holds his ground, for God will save.
Steel crosses wood, a flash, and oh!
Shame for beauty's overthrow!
(God's eyes are dim, His ears are shut.)
One cruel backhand sabre-cut —
'I'm hit! I'm killed!' young David cries,
Throws blindly forward, chokes . . . and dies.
And look, spike-helmeted, gray, grim,
Goliath straddles over him.

THE LAST POST

The bugler sent a call of high romance —
'Lights out! Lights out!' to the deserted square.
On the thin brazen notes he threw a prayer,
'God, if it's *this* for me next time in France . . .'
O spare the phantom bugle as I lie
Dead in the gas and smoke and roar of guns,
Dead in a row with the other broken ones
Lying so stiff and still under the sky,
Jolly young Fusiliers too good to die.'

WHEN I'M KILLED

When I'm killed, don't think of me
Buried there in Cambrin Wood,

Nor as in Zion think of me
With the Intolerable Good.
And there's one thing that I know well,
I'm damned if I'll be damned to Hell!

So when I'm killed, don't wait for me,
Walking the dim corridor;
In Heaven or Hell, don't wait for me,
Or you must wait for evermore.
You'll find me buried, living-dead
In these verses that you've read.

So when I'm killed, don't mourn for me,
Shot, poor lad, so bold and young,
Killed and gone — don't mourn for me.
On your lips my life is hung:
O friends and lovers, you can save
Your playfellow from the grave.

LETTER TO S. S. FROM MAMETZ WOOD

I never dreamed we'd meet that day
In our old haunts down Fricourt way,
Plotting such marvellous journeys there
For jolly old 'Après-la-guerre.'

Well, when it's over, first we'll meet
At Gweithdy Bach, my country seat
In Wales, a curious little shop
With two rooms and a roof on top,
A sort of Morlancourt-ish billet
That never needs a crowd to fill it.
But oh, the country round about!
The sort of view that makes you shout
For want of any better way
Of praising God: there's a blue bay
Shining in front, and on the right
Snowden and Hebog capped with white,
And lots of other jolly peaks
That you could wonder at for weeks,
With jag and spur and hump and cleft.
There's a gray castle on the left,

And back in the high Hinterland
You'll see the grave of Shawn Knarlbrand,
Who slew the savage Buffaloon
By the Nant-col one night in June,
And won his surname from the horn
Of this prodigious unicorn.
Beyond, where the two Rhinogs tower,
Rhinog Fach and Rhinog Fawr,
Close there after a four years' chase
From Thessaly and the woods of Thrace,
The beaten Dog-cat stood at bay
And growled and fought and passed away.
You'll see where mountain conies grapple
With prayer and creed in their rock chapel
Which Ben and Claire once built for them;
They call it Söar Bethlehem.
You'll see where in old Roman days,
Before Revivals changed our ways,
The Virgin 'scaped the Devil's grab,
Printing her foot on a stone slab
With five clear toe-marks; and you'll find
The fiendish thumbprint close behind.
You'll see where Math, Mathonwy's son,
Spoke with the wizard Gwydion
And bad him from South Wales set out
To steal that creature with the snout,
That new-discovered grunting beast
Divinely flavoured for the feast.
No traveller yet has hit upon
A wilder land than Meirion,
For desolate hills and tumbling stones,
Bogland and melody and old bones.
Fairies and ghosts are here galore,
And poetry most splendid, more
Than can be written with the pen
Or understood by common men.

In Gweithdy Bach we'll rest awhile,
We'll dress our wounds and learn to smile
With easier lips; we'll stretch our legs,
And live on bilberry tart and eggs,
And store up solar energy,

Basking in sunshine by the sea,
Until we feel a match once more
For *anything* but another war.

So then we'll kiss our families,
And sail across the seas
(The God of Song protecting us)
To the great hills of Caucasus.
Robert will learn the local *bat*
For billeting and things like that,
If Siegfried learns the piccolo
To charm the people as we go.

The jolly peasants clad in furs
Will greet the Welch-ski officers
With open arms, and ere we pass
Will make us vocal with Kavasse.
In old Bagdad we'll call a halt
At the Sâshuns' ancestral vault;
We'll catch the Persian rose-flowers' scent,
And understand what Omar meant.
Bitlis and Mush will know our faces,
Tiflis and Tomsk, and all such places.
Perhaps eventually we'll get
Among the Tartars of Thibet.
Hobnobbing with the Chungs and Mings,
And doing wild, tremendous things
In free adventure, quest and fight,
And God! what poetry we'll write!

A DEAD BOCHE

To you who'd read my songs of War
    And only hear of blood and fame,
I'll say (you've heard it said before)
    'War's Hell!' and if you doubt the same,
Today I found in Mametz Wood
A certain cure for lust of blood:

Where, propped against a shattered trunk,
    In a great mess of things unclean,
Sat a dead Boche; he scowled and stunk

With clothes and face a sodden green,
Big-bellied, spectacled, crop-haired,
Dribbling black blood from nose and beard.

THE NEXT WAR

You young friskies who today
Jump and fight in Father's hay
With bows and arrows and wooden spears,
Playing at Royal Welch Fusiliers,
Happy though these hours you spend,
Have they warned you how games end?
Boys, from the first time you prod
And thrust with spears of curtain-rod,
From the first time you tear and slash
Your long-bows from the garden ash,
Or fit your shaft with a blue jay feather,
Binding the split tops together,
From that same hour by fate you're bound
As champions of this stony ground,
Loyal and true in everything,
To serve your Army and your King,
Prepared to starve and sweat and die
Under some fierce foreign sky,
If only to keep safe those joys
That belong to British boys,
To keep young Prussians from the soft
Scented hay of father's loft,
And stop young Slavs from cutting bows
And bendy spears from Welsh hedgerows.
    Another War soon gets begun,
A dirtier, a more glorious one;
Then, boys, you'll have to play, all in;
It's the cruellest team will win.
So hold your nose against the stink
And never stop too long to think.
Wars don't change except in name;
The next one must go just the same,
And new foul tricks unguessed before
Will win and justify this War.
Kaisers and Czars will strut the stage
Once more with pomp and greed and rage;

Courtly ministers will stop
At home and fight to the last drop;
By the million men will die
In some new horrible agony;
And children here will thrust and poke,
Shoot and die, and laugh at the joke,
With bows and arrows and wooden spears,
Playing at Royal Welch Fusiliers.

ESCAPE

(*August* 6, 1916. — Officer previously reported died of wounds, now
reported wounded: Graves, Captain R., Royal Welch Fusiliers.)

. . . But I *was* dead, an hour or more.
I woke when I'd already passed the door
That Cerberus guards, and half-way down the road
To Lethe, as an old Greek signpost showed.
Above me, on my stretcher swinging by,
I saw new stars in the subterrene sky:
A Cross, a Rose in bloom, a Cage with bars,
And a barbed Arrow feathered in fine stars.
I felt the vapours of forgetfulness
Float in my nostrils. Oh, may Heaven bless
Dear Lady Proserpine, who saw me wake,
And, stooping over me, for Henna's sake
Cleared my poor buzzing head and sent me back
Breathless, with leaping heart along the track.
After me roared and clattered angry hosts
Of demons, heroes, and policeman-ghosts.
'Life! life! I can't be dead! I won't be dead!
Damned if I'll die for any one!' I said. . . .
Cerberus stands and grins above me now,
Wearing three heads — lion, and lynx, and sow.
'Quick, a revolver! But my Webley's gone,
Stolen! . . . No bombs . . . no knife. . . . The crowd swarms on,
Bellows, hurls stones. . . . Not even a honeyed sop . . .
Nothing. . . . Good Cerberus! . . . Good dog! . . . but stop!
Stay! . . . A great luminous thought . . . I do believe
There's still some morphia that I bought on leave.'
Then swiftly Cerberus' wide mouths I cram
With army biscuit smeared with ration jam;

And sleep lurks in the luscious plum and apple.
He crunches, swallows, stiffens, seems to grapple
With the all-powerful poppy . . . then a snore,
A crash; the beast blocks up the corridor
With monstrous hairy carcase, red and dun —
Too late! for I've sped through.
   O Life! O Sun!

THE BOUGH OF NONSENSE

AN IDYLL

 Back from the Somme two Fusiliers
 Limped painfully home; the elder said,
S. 'Robert, I've lived three thousand years
 This Summer, and I'm nine parts dead.'
R. 'But if that's truly so,' I cried, 'quick, now,
 Through these great oaks and see the famous bough

 'Where once a nonsense built her nest
 With skulls and flowers and all things queer,
 In an old boot, with patient breast
 Hatching three eggs; and the next year . . .'
S. 'Foaled thirteen squamous young beneath, and rid
 Wales of drink, melancholy, and psalms, she did.'

 Said he, 'Before this quaint mood fails,
 We'll sit and weave a nonsense hymn,'
R. 'Hanging it up with monkey tails
 In a deep grove all hushed and dim. . . .'
S. 'To glorious yellow-bunched banana-trees,'
R. 'Planted in dreams by pious Portuguese,'
S. 'Which men are wise beyond their time,

 And worship nonsense, no one more.'
R. 'Hard by, among old quince and lime,
 They've built a temple with no floor,'
S. 'And whosoever worships in that place,
 He disappears from sight and leaves no trace.'

R. 'Once the Galatians built a fane
 To Sense: what duller God than that?'
S. 'But the first day of autumn rain

The roof fell in and crushed them flat.'
R. 'Ay, for a roof of subtlest logic falls
   When nonsense is foundation for the walls.'

I tell him old Galatian tales;
He caps them in quick Portuguese,
While phantom creatures with green scales
Scramble and roll among the trees.
The hymn swells; on a bough above us sings
A row of bright pink birds, flapping their wings.

NOT DEAD

Walking through trees to cool my heat and pain,
I know that David's with me here again.
All that is simple, happy, strong, he is.
Caressingly I stroke
Rough bark of the friendly oak.
A brook goes bubbling by: the voice is his.
Turf burns with pleasant smoke;
I laugh at chaffinch and at primroses.
All that is simple, happy, strong, he is.
Over the whole wood in a little while
Breaks his slow smile.

THE ASSAULT HEROIC

Down in the mud I lay,
Tired out by my long day
Of five damned days and nights,
Five sleepless days and nights, . . .
Dream-snatched, and set me where
The dungeon of Despair
Looms over Desolate Sea,
Frowning and threatening me
With aspect high and steep —
A most malignant keep.
My foes that lay within
Shouted and made a din,
Hooted and grinned and cried:
'Today we've killed your pride;

Today your ardour ends.
We've murdered all your friends;
We've undermined by stealth
Your happiness and your health.
We've taken away your hope;
Now you may droop and mope
To misery and to Death.'
But with my spear of Faith,
Stout as an oaken rafter,
With my round shield of laughter,
With my sharp, tongue-like sword
That speaks a bitter word,
I stood beneath the wall
And there defied them all.
The stones they cast I caught
And alchemized with thought
Into such lumps of gold
As dreaming misers hold.
The boiling oil they threw
Fell in a shower of dew,
Refreshing me; the spears
Flew harmless by my ears,
Struck quivering in the sod;
There, like the prophet's rod,
Put leaves out, took firm root,
And bore me instant fruit.
My foes were all astounded,
Dumbstricken and confounded,
Gaping in a long row;
They dared not thrust nor throw.
Thus, then, I climbed a steep
Buttress and won the keep,
And laughed and proudly blew
My horn, 'Stand to! Stand to!
Wake up, sir! Here's a new
Attack! Stand to! Stand to!'

ALICE MEYNELL (1847–1922)

Born in Surrey, Alice Meynell was raised in Italy, France and Switzerland. The second daughter of a wealthy Englishman, Meynell received her education from her father. She published her first volume of poetry, *Preludes*, in 1875, and enjoyed the support of some of the greatest writers of the nineteenth century, such as John Ruskin, George Eliot and Christina Rossetti. In 1877, Meynell (née Thompson) married Wilfrid Meynell, a fellow writer, with whom she shared the journalistic work that contributed to their livelihood. Meynell was a social reformist, active in the women's suffrage movement and other causes. Meynell was 67 years old when the war broke out, and like all English civilians experienced the costs of the war: one of her sons-in-law died of wounds and her second son served in the military.

SUMMER IN ENGLAND, 1914

On London fell a clearer light;
    Caressing pencils of the sun
Defined the distances, the white
    Houses transfigured one by one,
The 'long, unlovely street' impearled.
O what a sky has waked the world!

Most happy year! And out of town
    The hay was prosperous, and the wheat;
The silken harvest climbed the down;
    Moon after moon was heavenly sweet,
Stroking the bread within the sheaves,
Looking twixt apples and their leaves.

And while this rose made round her cup,
    The armies died convulsed; and when
This chaste young silver sun went up
    Softly, a thousand shattered men,

One wet corruption, heaped the plain,
After a league-long throb of pain.

Flower following tender flower, and birds,
    And berries; and benignant skies
Made thrive the serried flocks and herds.
    Yonder are men shot through the eyes,
And children crushed. Love, hide thy face
From man's unpardonable race.

A REPLY

Who said 'No man hath greater love than this
    To die to serve his friend?'
So these have loved us all unto the end.
Chide thou no more, O thou unsacrificed!
The soldier dying dies upon a kiss,
The very kiss of Christ.

THOMAS HARDY (1840–1928)

Born near Dorchester, Thomas Hardy studied architecture before he turned to writing. In the early stages of his career he was primarily a novelist, and wrote such classic works as *Tess of the D'Urbervilles* (1891) and *Jude the Obscure* (1896). The latter turned out to be Hardy's last novel. Two years later, he published *Wessex Poems* and continued to write poetry rather than prose until his death. In his poetry as in his prose Hardy concentrated on the forces of fate and the imperviousness of nature, the individual's inability to control his or her destiny. The war poems in particular reflect Hardy's deep sense of irony, which seemed to be confirmed by the waste and horror of the war. John Crowe Ransom, commenting on Hardy's war poems, described " 'And There Was a Great Calm' " — written after Armistice Day — as "one of the noble war poems in our language, or any language."

CHANNEL FIRING

That night your great guns, unawares,
Shook all our coffins as we lay,
And broke the chancel window-squares,
We thought it was the Judgment-day

And sat upright. While drearisome
Arose the howl of wakened hounds:
The mouse let fall the altar-crumb,
The worms drew back into the mounds,

The glebe cow drooled. Till God called, 'No;
It's gunnery practice out at sea
Just as before you went below;
The world is as it used to be:

'All nations striving strong to make
Red war yet redder. Mad as hatters

They do no more for Christés sake
Than you who are helpless in such matters.

'That this is not the judgment-hour
For some of them's a blessed thing,
For if it were they'd have to scour
Hell's floor for so much threatening. . . .

'Ha, ha. It will be warmer when
I blow the trumpet (if indeed
I ever do; for you are men,
And rest eternal sorely need).'

So down we lay again, 'I wonder,
Will the world ever saner be,'
Said one, 'than when He sent us under
In our indifferent century!'

And many a skeleton shook his head.
'Instead of preaching forty year,'
My neighbour Parson Thirdly said,
'I wish I had stuck to pipes and beer.'

Again the guns disturbed the hour,
Roaring their readiness to avenge,
As far inland as Stourton Tower,
And Camelot, and starlit Stonehenge.

SONG OF THE SOLDIERS

What of the faith and fire within us
        Men who march away
        Ere the barn-cocks say
        Night is growing gray,
To hazards whence no tears can win us;
What of the faith and fire within us
        Men who march away?

Is it a purblind prank, O think you,
        Friend with the musing eye
        Who watch us stepping by,
        With doubt and dolorous sigh?

Can much pondering so hoodwink you!
Is it a purblind prank, O think you,
    Friend with the musing eye?

Nay. We see well what we are doing,
    Though some may not see —
    Dalliers as they be! —
    England's need are we;
Her distress would set us ruing:
Nay. We see well what we are doing,
    Though some may not see!

In our heart of hearts believing
    Victory crowns the just,
    And that braggarts must
    Surely bite the dust,
March we to the field ungrieving,
In our heart of hearts believing
    Victory crowns the just.

Hence the faith and fire within us
    Men who march away
    Ere the barn-cocks say
    Night is growing gray,
To hazards whence no tears can win us;
Hence the faith and fire within us
    Men who march away.

BELGIUM'S DESTITUTE*

AN APPEAL TO AMERICA

    Seven millions stand
Emaciate, in that ancient Delta-land: —
We here, full charged with our own maimed and dead,
And coiled in throbbing conflicts slow and sore,
Can soothe how slight these ails unmerited
Of souls forlorn upon the facing shore!
Where naked, gaunt, in endless band on band
    Seven millions stand.

---

* This poem, written as an appeal to the American people on behalf of the destitute people of Belgium, was given out by the American Commission for Relief in Belgium, January 3, 1915.

No man can say
To your great country that, with scant delay,
You must, perforce, ease them in their sore need:
We know that nearer first your duty lies;
But — is it much to ask that you let plead
Your loving kindness with you — wooing wise —
Albeit that aught you owe and must repay
No man can say?

BEFORE MARCHING, AND AFTER

(In Memoriam: F. W. G.)

Orion swung southward aslant
Where the starved Egdon pine-trees had thinned,
The Pleiads aloft seemed to pant
With the heather that twitched in the wind;
But he looked on indifferent to sights such as these,
Unswayed by love, friendship, home joy or home sorrow,
And wondered to what he would march on the morrow.

The crazed household clock with its whirr
Rang midnight within as he stood,
He heard the low sighing of her
Who had striven from his birth for his good;
But he still only asked the spring starlight, the breeze,
What great thing or small thing his history would borrow
From that Game with Death he would play on the morrow.

When the heath wore the robe of late summer,
And the fuchsia-bells, hot in the sun,
Hung red by the door, a quick comer
Brought tidings that marching was done
For him who had joined in that game overseas
Where Death stood to win; though his memory would borrow
A brightness therefrom not to die on the morrow.

IN TIME OF 'THE BREAKING OF NATIONS'

I.

Only a man harrowing clods
    In a slow silent walk
With an old horse that stumbles and nods
    Half asleep as they stalk.

II.

Only thin smoke without flame
    From the heaps of couch grass;
— Yet this will go on just the same
    Tho' dynasties pass.

III.

Yonder a maid and her wight
    Come whispering by;
War's annals will fade into night
    Ere their story die.

THE PITY OF IT

I walked in loamy Wessex lanes, afar
From rail-track and from highway, and I heard
In field and farmstead many an ancient word
Of local lineage like 'Thu bist,' 'Er war,'
'Ich woll,' 'Er sholl,' and by-talk similar,
Nigh as they speak who in this month's moon gird
At England's very loins, thereunto spurred
By gangs whose glory threats and slaughters are.
Then seemed a Heart crying: 'Whosoever they be
At root and bottom of this, who flung this flame
Between kin folk kin tongued even as are we,

'Sinister, ugly, lurid, be their fame;
May their familiars grow to shun their name,
And their brood perish everlastingly.'

THEN AND NOW

When battles were fought
With a chivalrous sense of should and ought,
    In spirit men said,

'End we quick or dead,
        Honour is some reward!
Let us fight fair — for our own best or worst;
        So, Gentlemen of the Guard,
            Fire first!'

        In the open they stood,
Man to man in his knightlihood:
        They would not deign
        To profit by a stain
        On the honourable rules,
Knowing that practise perfidy no man durst
        Who in the heroic schools
            Was nurst.

        But now, behold, what
Is war with those where honour is not!
        Rama laments
        Its dead innocents;
        Herod howls: 'Sly slaughter
Rules now! Let us, by modes once called accurst,
        Overhead, under water,
            Stab first.'

'AND THERE WAS A GREAT CALM'

(ON THE SIGNING OF THE ARMISTICE, NOVEMBER 11, 1918)

There had been years of Passion — scorching, cold,
And much Despair, and Anger heaving high,
Care whitely watching. Sorrows manifold,
Among the young, among the weak and old,
And the pensive Spirit of Pity whispered, 'Why?'

Men had not paused to answer. Foes distraught
Pierced the thinned peoples in a brute-like blindness,
Philosophies that sages long had taught,
And Selflessness, were as an unknown thought,
And 'Hell!' and 'Shell!' were yapped at Lovingkindness.

The feeble folk at home had grown full-used
To 'dug-outs,' 'snipers,' 'Huns,' from the war-adept

In the mornings heard, and at evetides perused;
To day-dreamt men in millions, when they mused —
To nightmare-men in millions when they slept.

Waking to wish existence timeless, null,
Sirius they watched above where armies fell;
He seemed to check his flapping when, in the lull
Of night a boom came thencewise, like the dull
Plunge of a stone dropped into some deep well.

So, when old hopes that earth was bettering slowly
Were dead and damned, there sounded 'War is done!'
One morrow. Said the bereft, and meek, and lowly,
'Will men some day be given to grace? yea, wholly,
And in good sooth, as our dreams used to run?'

Breathless they paused. Out there men raised their glance
To where had stood those poplars lank and lopped,
As they had raised it through the four years' dance
Of Death in the now familiar flats of France;
And murmured, 'Strange, this! How? All firing stopped?'

Aye; all was hushed. The about-to-fire fired not,
The aimed-at moved away in trance-lipped song.
One checkless regiment slung a clinching shot
And turned. The Spirit of Irony smirked out, 'What?
Spoil peradventures woven of Rage and Wrong?'

Thenceforth no flying fires inflamed the gray,
No hurtlings shook the dewdrop from the thorn,
No moan perplexed the mute bird on the spray;
Worn horses mused: 'We are not whipped to-day';
No weft-winged engines blurred the moon's thin horn.

Calm fell. From Heaven distilled a clemency;
There was peace on earth, and silence in the sky;
Some could, some could not, shake off misery:
The Sinister Spirit sneered: 'It had to be!'
And again the Spirit of Pity whispered, 'Why?'

ROBERT BRIDGES (1844–1930)

Robert Bridges was educated at Eton and later at Corpus Christi College, Oxford. He studied medicine at St. Bartholemew's Hospital in London and became a practicing physician. Poetry, however, was Bridges' true vocation, and after retiring from medicine in 1882 and publishing many volumes of poetry and criticism, he was appointed Poet Laureate in 1913. Bridges is not often anthologized today; his most lasting gift to English letters was the rescue of the poetry of Gerard Manley Hopkins from obscurity. "To the United States of America" was occasioned by the United States' entry into the war in 1917.

TO THE UNITED STATES OF AMERICA

Brothers in blood! They who this wrong began
  To wreck our commonwealth, will rue the day
   When first they challenged freemen to the fray,
And with the Briton dared the American.
Now are we pledged to win the Rights of man;
  Labour and Justice now shall have their way,
   And in a League of Peace — God grant we may —
Transform the earth, not patch up the old plan.

Sure is our hope since he who led your nation
  Spake for mankind, and ye arose in awe
Of that high call to work the world's salvation;
    Clearing your minds of all estranging blindness
  In the vision of Beauty and the Spirit's law,
    Freedom and Honour and sweet Lovingkindness.

TRAFALGAR SQUARE

Fool that I was! my heart was sore,
Yea, sick for the myriad wounded men,
The maim'd in the war: I had grief for each one:

And I came in the gay September sun
To the open smile of Trafalgar Square,
Where many a lad with a limb foredone
Loll'd by the lion-guarded column
That holdeth Nelson statued thereon
Upright in the air.

The Parliament towers, and the Abbey towers,
The white Horseguards and gray Whitehall,
He looketh on all,
Past Somerset House and the river's bend
To the pillar'd dome of St. Paul,
That slumbers, confessing God's solemn blessing
On Britain's glory, to keep it ours —
While children true her prowess renew
And throng from the ends of the earth to defend
Freedom and honour — till Earth shall end.

The gentle unjealous Shakespeare, I trow,
In his country grave of peaceful fame
Must feel exiled from life and glow,
If he thinks of this man with his warrior claim,
Who looketh on London as if 't were his own,
As he standeth in stone, aloft and alone,
Sailing the sky, with one arm and one eye.

A. E. HOUSMAN (1859–1936)

Alfred Edward Housman was born in Worcestershire and studied at Oxford University. A student of the classics, Housman failed his final examinations, but continued to pursue his studies of Latin and Greek, contributing to scholarly journals. In 1892 he was named to the Chair of Latin at University College in London, and from there moved to Cambridge, where he served as a professor of Latin from 1911 until 1936. During his lifetime, Housman published two volumes of poetry, *A Shropshire Lad* (1896) and *Last Poems* (1922). Housman's most famous "war poem," "Epitaph on an Army of Mercenaries," was composed in honor of the third anniversary of the First Battle of Ypres (1914) and printed in *The Times* on October 31, 1917. The poet Hugh MacDiarmid wrote a response, "Another Epitaph on an Army of Mercenaries" (1935), in which he calls Housman's valorization of the professional soldiers a "God-damned lie," and describes the mercenaries themselves — members of the British Regular Army — as "professional murderers." Housman had a more positive influence on Charles Sorley and Ivor Gurney, who exhibited a similar sense of irony and resignation while avoiding, like Housman, any tendency toward self-pity.

EPITAPH ON AN ARMY OF MERCENARIES

These, in the day when heaven was falling,
  The hour when earth's foundations fled,
Followed their mercenary calling
  And took their wages and are dead.

Their shoulders held the sky suspended;
  They stood, and earth's foundations stay;
What God abandoned, these defended,
  And saved the sum of things for pay.

RUDYARD KIPLING (1865–1936)

Although Rudyard Kipling is usually viewed as a staunch defender of the British Empire, his stance toward imperialism should not be oversimplified. In much of his writing, poetry and prose, his characters — oftentimes the anonymous men sent to enforce British rule in India — appear powerless to change the course of imperialism. Kipling's talent for portraying the "common" man made him one of the best-loved poets in England; his work carried a great deal of popular appeal and his influences ranged from the classical traditions of English poetry to music-hall lyrics to Methodist hymns. The poems that Kipling wrote in response to World War One reveal the strains of his sympathetic popular sentiment, and many echo the fierce anti-German propaganda of the period. Despite Kipling's patriotism and allegiance to what he considered the Englishman's duty, however, he was not insensitive to the horrors of the war, nor did he blindly accept the political rhetoric that called for needless human sacrifice, as shown by "A Dead Statesman":

> I could not dig; I dared not rob;
> Therefore I lied to please the mob.
> Now all my lies are proved untrue
> And I must face the men I slew.
> What tale shall serve me here among
> Mine angry and defrauded young?

THE MINE-SWEEPERS

Dawn off the Foreland — the young flood making
　　Jumbled and short and steep —
Black in the hollows and bright where it's breaking —
　　Awkward water to sweep.
　　'Mines reported in the fairway,
　　Warn all traffic and detain.
Sent up *Unity, Claribel, Assyrian, Stormcock,* and *Golden Gain.'*

Noon off the Foreland — the first ebb making
   Lumpy and strong in the bight.
Boom after boom, and the golf-hut shaking
   And the jackdaws wild with fright.
   'Mines located in the fairway,
   Boats now working up the chain,
Sweepers — *Unity, Claribel, Assyrian, Stormcock,* and *Golden Gain.*'

Dusk off the Foreland — the last light going
   And the traffic crowding through,
And five damned trawlers with their syreens blowing
   Heading the whole review!
   'Sweep completed in the fairway.
   No more mines remain.
Sent back *Unity, Claribel, Assyrian, Stormcock,* and *Golden Gain.*'

'FOR ALL WE HAVE AND ARE'

For all we have and are,
For all our children's fate,
Stand up and meet the war.
The Hun is at the gate!
Our world has passed away
In wantonness o'erthrown.
There is nothing left to-day
But steel and fire and stone.

     Though all we knew depart,
     The old commandments stand:
     'In courage keep your heart,
     In strength lift up your hand.'

Once more we hear the word
That sickened earth of old:
'No law except the sword
Unsheathed and uncontrolled,'
Once more it knits mankind,
Once more the nations go
To meet and break and bind
A crazed and driven foe.

Comfort, content, delight —
The ages' slow-bought gain —
They shrivelled in a night,
Only ourselves remain
To face the naked days
In silent fortitude,
Through perils and dismays
Renewed and re-renewed.

Though all we made depart,
The old commandments stand:
'In patience keep your heart,
In strength lift up your hand.'

No easy hopes or lies
Shall bring us to our goal,
But iron sacrifice
Of body, will, and soul
There is but one task for all —
For each one life to give.
Who stands if freedom fall?
Who dies if England live?

THE CHOICE

THE AMERICAN SPIRIT SPEAKS:

To the Judge of Right and Wrong
    With Whom fulfillment lies
Our purpose and our power belong,
    Our faith and sacrifice.

Let Freedom's land rejoice!
    Our ancient bonds are riven;
Once more to us the eternal choice
    Of good or ill is given.

Not at a little cost,
    Hardly by prayer or tears,
Shall we recover the road we lost
    In the drugged and doubting years.

But after the fires and the wrath,
  But after searching and pain,
His Mercy opens us a path
  To live with ourselves again.

In the Gates of Death rejoice!
  We see and hold the good —
Bear witness, Earth, we have made our choice
  For Freedom's brotherhood.

Then praise the Lord Most High
  Whose Strength hath saved us whole,
Who bade us choose that the Flesh should die
  And not the living Soul!

WALTER DE LA MARE (1873–1956)

The son of a naval surgeon, Walter de la Mare was educated at St. Paul's School. At 17, he joined the offices of the Standard Oil Company as a bookkeeper, though he considered himself a writer. In 1908 he was awarded a government pension, at which time he was able to pursue his literary interests full time. Like most of the noncombatant poets in this collection, de la Mare felt compelled to address the issues surrounding the war through verse. Two such poems are presented here, "The Fool Rings His Bells" and " 'How Sleep the Brave.' "

THE FOOL RINGS HIS BELLS

Come, Death, I'd have a word with thee;
And thou, poor Innocency;
And Love — a lad with broken wing;
And Pity, too:
The Fool shall sing to you,
As Fools will sing.

Ay, music hath small sense,
And a tune's soon told,
And Earth is old,
And my poor wits are dense;
Yet have I secrets, — dark, my dear,
To breathe you all: Come near.
And lest some hideous listener tells,
I'll ring my bells.

They're all at war!
Yes, yes, their bodies go
'Neath burning sun and icy star
To chaunted songs of woe,
Dragging cold cannon through a mud
Of rain and blood;

66

The new moon glinting hard on eyes
Wide with insanities!

Hush! . . . I use words
I hardly know the meaning of;
And the mute birds
Are glancing at Love!
From out their shade of leaf and flower,
Trembling at treacheries
Which even in noonday cower.
Heed, heed not what I said
Of frenzied hosts of men,
More fools than I,
On envy, hatred fed,
Who kill, and die —
Spake I not plainly, then?
Yet Pity whispered, 'Why?'

Thou silly thing, off to thy daisies go.
Mine was not news for child to know,
And Death — no ears hath. He hath supped where creep
Eyeless worms in hush of sleep;
Yet, when he smiles, the hand he draws
Athwart his grinning jaws
Faintly their thin bones rattle, and. . . . There, there;
Hearken how my bells in the air
Drive away care! . . .

Nay, but a dream I had
Of a world all mad.
Not a simple happy mad like me,
Who am mad like an empty scene
Of water and willow tree,
Where the wind hath been;
But that foul Satan-mad,
Who rots in his own head,
And counts the dead,
Not honest one — and two —
But for the ghosts they were,
Brave, faithful, true,

When, head in air,
In Earth's clear green and blue
Heaven they did share
With Beauty who bade them there. . . .

There, now! he goes —
Old Bones; I've wearied him.
Ay, and the light doth dim,
And asleep's the rose,
And tired Innocence
In dreams is hence. . . .
Come, Love, my lad,
Nodding that drowsy head,
'Tis time thy prayers were said!

'HOW SLEEP THE BRAVE'

Nay, nay, sweet England, do not grieve!
    Not one of these poor men who died
But did within his soul believe
    That death for thee was glorified.

Ever they watched it hovering near
    That mystery 'yond thought to plumb,
Perchance sometimes in loathèd fear
    They heard cold Danger whisper, Come! —

Heard and obeyed. O, if thou weep
    Such courage and honour, beauty, care,
Be it for joy that those who sleep
    Only thy joy could share.

MAY WEDDERBURN CANNAN (1893–1973)

May Wedderburn Cannan was raised and educated in Oxford, where her father was an executive for Oxford University Press. Cannan was already working as a Red Cross volunteer when England entered the war, and she continued her work with the Red Cross until 1918, when she joined the War Office in Paris. Unlike much poetry written by women during this period, Cannan's reveals a closer perspective of the effects of the war than that of her counterparts who remained at home. She had worked as a volunteer in a military canteen in Rouen, France, in the spring of 1915, and what she saw there convinced her that it was her duty to support those soldiers who believed their cause to be just.

ROUEN

26 April–25 May 1915

Early morning over Rouen, hopeful, high, courageous morning,
And the laughter of adventure and the steepness of the stair,
And the dawn across the river, and the wind across the bridges,
And the empty littered station and the tired people there.

Can you recall those mornings and the hurry of awakening,
And the long-forgotten wonder if we should miss the way,
And the unfamiliar faces, and the coming of provisions,
And the freshness and the glory of the labour of the day?

Hot noontide over Rouen, and the sun upon the city,
Sun and dust unceasing, and the glare of cloudless skies,
And the voices of the Indians and the endless stream of soldiers,
And the clicking of the tatties, and the buzzing of the flies.

Can you recall those noontides and the reek of steam and coffee,
Heavy-laden noontides with the evening's peace to win,
And the little piles of Woodbines, and the sticky soda bottles,
And the crushes in the 'Parlour,' and the letters coming in?

Quiet night-time over Rouen, and the station full of soldiers,
All the youth and pride of England from the ends of all the earth;
And the rifles piled together, and the creaking of the sword-belts,
And the faces bent above them, and the gay, heart-breaking mirth.

Can I forget the passage from the cool white-bedded Aid Post
Past the long sun-blistered coaches of the khaki Red Cross train
To the truck train full of wounded, and the weariness and laughter,
And 'Good-bye, and thank-you, Sister,' and the empty yards again?

Can you recall the parcels that we made them for the railroad,
Crammed and bulging parcels held together by their string,
And the voices of the sergeants who called the Drafts together,
And the agony and splendour when they stood to save the King?

Can you forget their passing, the cheering and the waving,
The little group of people at the doorway of the shed,
The sudden awful silence when the last train swung to darkness,
And the lonely desolation, and the mocking stars o'erhead?

Can you recall the midnights, and the footsteps of night watchers,
Men who came from darkness and went back to dark again,
And the shadows on the rail-lines and the all-inglorious labour,
And the promise of the daylight firing blue the window-pane?

Can you recall the passing through the kitchen door to morning,
Morning very still and solemn breaking slowly on the town,
And the early coastways engines that had met the ships at daybreak,
And the Drafts just out from England, and the day shift coming down?

Can you forget returning slowly, stumbling on the cobbles,
And the white-decked Red Cross barges dropping seawards for the tide,
And the search for English papers, and the blessed cool of water,
And the peace of half-closed shutters that shut out the world outside?

Can I forget the evenings and the sunsets on the island,
And the tall black ships at anchor far below our balcony,
And the distant call of bugles, and the white wine in the glasses,
And the long line of the street lamps, stretching Eastwards to the sea?

. . . When the world slips slow to darkness, when the office fire burns
    lower,
My heart goes out to Rouen, Rouen all the world away;
When other men remember I remember our Adventure
And the trains that go from Rouen at the ending of the day.